Build References Not Facades

4 Metal facade secrets That make projects Talk-worthy

Build References Not Facades

4 Metal facade secrets That make projects Talk-worthy

ANKUR HORA

Available on amazonkindle

Worldwide Published by

Pendown Press
PREMIUM BUSINESS PUBLISHER

PENDOWN PRESS LLP

An ISO 9001 & ISO 14001 Certified Co.,

Regd. Office: 3767A, Kanhaiya Nagar,
Tri Nagar, Delhi-110035
Ph.: 8130886000, 9650072927
E-mail: info@pendownpress.com
Branch Office: 1A/2A, 20, Hari Sadan, Ansari Road,
Daryaganj, New Delhi-110002
Ph.: 011-45794768
Website: PendownPress.com

Edition: 2026
Price: ₹ ~~1998~~ 269
ISBN: 978-93-7217-560-8

Layout and Cover Designed by Pendown Graphics Team

Table of Content

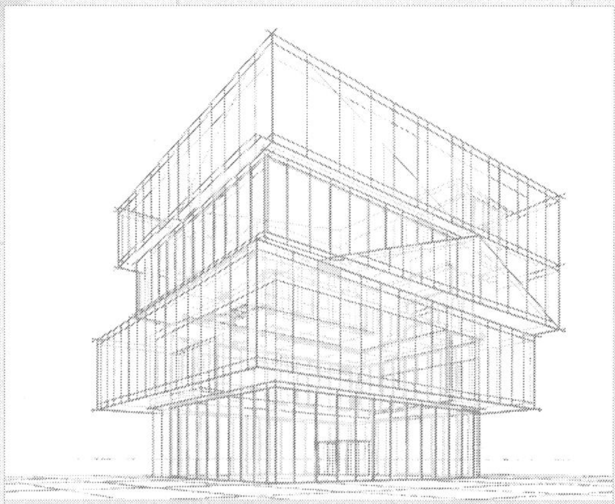

Prologue

Opening With Love and Gratitude

Every building begins with a foundation, and so does every life.

This book may carry my voice, but its strength comes from the people who have shaped me, anchored me, challenged me, and stood beside me at every step of the journey.

To Aastha, my wife. You are the quiet certainty in every uncertain day. Your patience, your steadiness, and your unwavering belief have been the invisible scaffolding behind every project, every risk, every idea that I dared to chase. You are the calm in my ambition and the reason I can build without fear.

To my parents, Amrit and Suman. Everything I know about discipline, humility, and responsibility began with you. You taught me that work has meaning only when it is done with sincerity, that success matters only when it carries integrity, and that the world notices silence just as much as achievement. This book is a reflection of the values you lived, not only the ones you spoke.

To my children, Vivann and Vedikka. You are the future I am building toward. Every line I draw, every facade I resolve, every idea I protect carries a silent hope that you will grow up in cities that feel dignified, grounded, and full of intention. May you always build lives that feel true to who you are, the same way I try to build structures that stay true to what they were meant to become.

This book is because of you and for all of you.

My foundation.

My clarity.

My greatest source of purpose.

Your design is not the problem. Execution is.

Here Is How You Take Back Control.

Architects do not struggle with ideas.

They struggle with everything that happens after the idea is approved.

You already know how to design a façade that works.

You already understand proportion, rhythm, joints, grids, and light. You already see the final building in your head long before anyone else does.

Your problem is not design.

Your problem is the number of things outside your control that quietly pull your design apart.

You know this feeling.

A façade that looked perfect in the drawing ends up looking slightly off in real life.

- A detail that was meant to stay crisp ends up looking improvised.
- A grid that was aligned perfectly on your plans suddenly shifts at the site.
- A finish that was meant to stay consistent loses shade because of production issues.
- A joint detail that depended on concealed fixings becomes exposed due to rushed installation.

Your façade was not designed wrongly.

Your façade was executed incorrectly.

This book is here to help you stop that from happening.

Most of this happens because critical metal façade decisions are taken late, without full awareness of how execution factors compound over time.

It is not about teaching architecture. You already know architecture.

It is about giving you:

- The **technical clarity,**
- The **metal façade**
- The **production insight**
- And **execution control** that most architects are never given access to.

Here is what this book will solve for you by building the right metal façade awareness across design, production, and execution:

- How missing metal façade awareness and delayed decisions quietly trigger execution failures later → Why façade materials behave differently on site compared to how they behave in your model
- How structural grids, bracket logic, offsets, and tolerances quietly influence the final look
- How to prevent vendors from cutting corners in production
- How to lock façade decisions so clients cannot force costly and damaging changes later
- How to choose coatings, metals, and grades that protect both the look and the lifespan

- How to eliminate failures during installation
- How to maintain design intent from the first sketch to the final panel

If you have ever thought, "This is not what I designed," this book will finally explain why that happened and how to make sure it does not happen again.

You do not need more theory.

You need a practical, margin-based, detail-based, site-based guide that protects your work.

That is what this book is.

- It will show you what leads to distortion, misalignment, warping, fading, cracking, buckling, and inconsistency.
- It will show you how to prevent these problems before they ever reach the site. It will give you a clear, step-by-step understanding of how façades succeed only when planning, products, production, and execution all speak the same language.
- Most importantly, it will allow you to regain control over what happens after your drawings leave your desk.

Your design is solid.

Your intent is clear.

This book helps you protect both.

Let us begin.

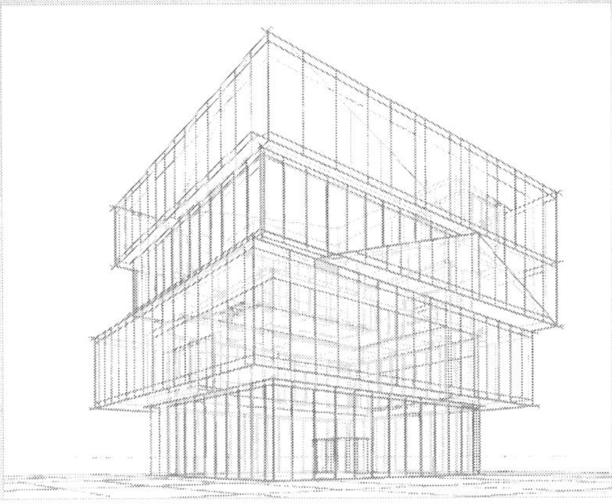

PART I
The Reality Architects Face

Chapter 1

The Silent Death of Design

There is a moment every architect knows too well.

The concept is locked. The client is aligned. The drawings are frozen. Your internal team feels satisfied because the design finally looks exactly the way it should. The massing is balanced. The grid is clean. The joints behave. The proportions sit comfortably. The façade feels like an honest extension of the building's intent.

And then the drawings leave your office.

That is the moment architecture stops being an idea and becomes a negotiation with reality.

- No one teaches this in architecture school.
- No one warns you about the number of people who will unknowingly chip away at your design.
- No one tells you that the most dangerous stage for your façade is not the beginning. It is everything that happens after the GFC is issued.

Once the project reaches the execution ecosystem, your design enters a world with its own physics, its own priorities, compromises, and mistakes waiting to happen.

Most of this erosion begins when metal façade decisions are deferred or taken without full awareness of how execution factors compound later.

The ecosystem where your design begins to erode

A façade is not executed in one straight line.

It is built in a crowded intersection where multiple teams make independent decisions, rarely in full sync with one another.

Here is what actually happens behind the scenes:

- **The structural team modifies beam or column placement** based on site constraints, leading to bracket exposure or broken façade alignment.
- **The MEP team shifts ducts, vents**, and drainage lines without checking their impact on your façade grid.
- **The site contractor improvises** because something does not fit, and he is running behind schedule.
- **The façade vendor changes the alloy grade** because the originally specified grade is not available or is costlier.
- **The production unit uses a fresh batch of coating powder** because the previous batch ran out, causing shade variation.
- **The installer starts work from the wrong end of the building** because it feels faster, causing the entire joint rhythm to go off.
- **The client asks for a last-minute functional change** without knowing how many steps will collapse as a result.

None of these decisions carries malicious intent.

Yet each one quietly distorts your design.

What you drew and what gets built begin drifting apart layer by layer until one day you stand on site, look up at the façade, and feel a familiar pain in your stomach. This is not what you designed.

- You know it.
- You see it.
- You feel it.

But you also know you did not have control over the processes that led to this outcome.

The Real Reason Good Façades Fail

Architects are often blamed for decisions they never made.

Most façade failures are not conceptual. They are workflow failures caused by missing metal façade awareness. Alignment failures. Communication failures. Production failures. Tolerance failures. Coating failures. Sequencing failures.

A façade is a system, not a surface.

And any system that is not guarded collapses under pressure.

This is why MetaMask stepped into the façade ecosystem.

- Not to replace architects.
- Not to challenge design.
- But to protect it.

"The design never fails on paper. The design fails because no one guarded its journey from the studio to the site."

- Ankur Hora, Founder of MetaMask

This single line captures the reality of the Indian construction environment better than any technical textbook.

- Designers create clarity.
- Execution environments create distortion.
- Between the two lies a gap that no one controls.

That gap widens when metal façade decisions are delayed and execution realities are addressed too late.

That gap is where your façade dies.

Why This Book Matters

This book does not tell you what architecture is.

You already know that.

This book gives you what no one else has given you:

Clear visibility of every metal façade point at which your façade can go wrong, and the exact steps to prevent it.

You will understand:

- Where the first cracks in alignment start
- Why façade systems fail even with perfect drawings
- How planning mistakes quietly become execution nightmares
- How wrong alloys, coatings, and grids ruin material behavior
- Why production shortcuts destroy panel quality
- How installers unknowingly damage the final aesthetic
- How marginal tolerances create monumental visual errors
- How timelines, sequencing, and site pressure break façade intent
- How to preserve your design even when ten different teams are pulling it apart

When you understand these hidden forces, you stop fighting fires at the site and start preventing them months earlier.

Architects do not need more inspiration.

Architects need deeper control over metal façades.

That control begins with understanding how metal façades actually behave. **This book hands that control back to you through metal façade clarity. You will be able to:**

- Understand metal façades well enough to freeze decisions with confidence.
- Demand the right QC processes.
- Identify production risks caused by wrong metal façade choices before fabrication.
- Reject wrong details before they reach the site.
- Align structural, MEP, lighting, and façade logic early.
- Anticipate problems that vendors cannot see.
- Protect your design through the entire journey.

Most importantly, you will no longer be blamed for mistakes that were never yours.

Your design is sound.

Your intent is clear.

This book protects both.

KEY TAKEAWAYS

- Designs in metal façades fail in execution, not in drawings.
- Architects lose control once multiple teams start making independent decisions. Structural, MEP, production, and installation errors quietly distort metal façade design intent.

- Metal façade failures are workflow failures, not conceptual failures.
- The Indian metal façade ecosystem lacks coordination and protection for your design.

MetaMask exists to guard your design through planning, production, and execution. Understanding these hidden forces gives architects control over outcomes.

Chapter 2

Why Common Façade Materials Limit Your Vision

Every architect begins a façade with a clear idea of what the building should communicate. You imagine the massing, the rhythm, the joints, the shadows, the light, and the surface language. The intent is always strong. The story is always clear.

Then the material selection process begins, and suddenly the entire façade starts responding to rules you did not write.

- HPL appears safe, but it behaves differently under heat.
- ACP looks polished in brochures, but develops waviness and oil canning once installed on a less-than-perfect substructure.
- Stone feels solid until moisture, weight, and fixing details start dictating how much freedom you truly have.
- Glass demands structural precision that is rarely present on site.
- Terracotta has charm but arrives with firing variations and strict sizing. GRC carries expressive potential but cracks easily when tolerances shift. Wood and WPC look warm on day one and unpredictable by year two.

The problem here is not design skill.

The challenge lies in the mismatch between what the architect imagines and what the material can deliver in real-world Indian conditions.

The Invisible Ceiling on Creativity

The geometry looks perfect in the model, but once the façade team begins aligning it with the material's capabilities, compromises start appearing.

- Modules dictate panel sizes.
- Weight dictates form.
- Fixing systems dictates visibility.
- Weather dictates lifespan.
- Manufacturing dictates what curves are possible.

Slowly and quietly, the material begins redesigning the façade on your behalf.

You are not changing the design because it was weak.

You are changing it because the material is rigid.

Many architects have watched a beautiful idea lose its sharpness simply because the chosen material could not bend, curve, stretch, or behave the way the design required. The façade that was supposed to feel precise ends up looking adjusted. The shadow lines shift. The joint rhythm breaks. The clean geometry gets softened in ways you never intended.

Material Behavior that Drawings Do Not Reveal

When a façade is executed, every material begins to reveal its character. Some expand. Some contract. Some warp. Some fade. Some crack. Some show fixing marks. Some resist moisture poorly. Some react badly to heat. Some struggle with coastal conditions. Some require such tight tolerances that the site team simply cannot match them.

No brochure speaks openly about these things.

No vendor presentation highlights these constraints.

No specification sheet warns you about the level of alignment required for perfection. Architects face the consequences without ever being shown the full picture.

What begins as a design intention quietly becomes a negotiation with material behavior.

Where Frustration Builds

Every architect has had moments where the result looks slightly off from the original intention, yet no single person can be blamed.

The cause is distributed across:

The nature of the material... the production process... the limitations of the fixing systems... climate sensitivity... installation conditions... and the way the site adjusts things in real time

You know what the façade should look like.

You can see the difference immediately.

But you are forced to accept the outcome because the material simply did not cooperate.

This is the part of the profession no one discusses openly.

Why This Matters Before You Choose the Next Façade

A material is not just a surface.

It is a decision that defines what your façade can and cannot do.

Once a material is chosen, it begins to act like a boundary.

It controls geometry, expression, depth, openings, shadows, lighting, fusion with other materials, maintenance cycles, and the overall experience of the building.

You are not choosing a product.

You are choosing the limits of your own imagination.

This chapter is not asking you to reject traditional materials.

They all have their place.

They all have their strengths.

But when the goal is expressive freedom, long-term stability, or a façade that must carry a sophisticated identity, these materials often force you to fight a battle you cannot win.

> "Façade performance is ultimately defined by material behaviour, not by conceptual clarity alone."
>
> **- Ankur Hora, Founder of MetaMask**

This is the truth behind most façade frustrations.

Understanding it is the first step toward choosing materials that support your vision instead of restraining it.

Key Takeaways

- Most traditional façade materials come with restrictions that only appear during execution.
- These materials limit geometry, module sizing, lighting integration, and long-term aesthetic stability.

- Design intent weakens not because of poor design but because of material behavior in real conditions.
- Once you choose a material, it becomes the boundary within which your creativity must operate.

Knowing these limitations helps you choose materials that align with the intensity of your vision.

Chapter 3

The Six Universal Failures Across Traditional Façade Materials

Every architect eventually reaches a point where the façade they imagined and the façade they receive begin to drift apart.

It is never one big mistake that causes the shift. It is a series of small, predictable limitations that live inside the material system itself.

These limitations are quiet at first.

- They make no noise on drawings.
- They show no warning signs in presentations.
- They remain invisible until the execution stage begins, revealing them one by one.

The truth is simple.

Traditional façade materials were never designed for the level of freedom, precision, and identity that contemporary architecture demands today.

They were built for stability and standardization, not expression. Which is why, when an architect attempts a sharper grid, a deeper reveal, a subtler shadow, or a more complex massing logic, the material begins resisting long before the façade reaches the site.

This resistance is not the result of inexperience or poor detailing.

It is the natural outcome of the six universal failures embedded in almost every conventional façade material used in India.

You already know these failures exist because you have seen the symptoms countless times. What this chapter will do is show you the root cause behind those symptoms and help you understand why every traditional material eventually behaves the same way.

Form Restriction: Where Creativity Runs Into a Wall

Every façade begins with an idea of form. The lines you draw, the surface language you imagine, the play of shadows you want to create, all originate from that first moment of creative clarity. Traditional materials interrupt that clarity very early in the process.

The problem begins when the material forces you into flatness.

- **HPL** cannot curve beyond a limit.
- **ACP** can bend only at specific radii and with specific tools.
- **Stone** refuses to accept nuanced shapes because its weight makes anything delicate unsafe.
- **Terracotta** restricts you to modules.
- **GRC** allows more freedom but cracks under pressure if tolerances shift.
- **Glass** needs structured support and cannot achieve sculptural expression without heavy hardware.

This means the moment you push beyond what the material is comfortable doing, you end up redesigning the façade, not because the design was flawed, but because the material is unwilling to cooperate. You are not just choosing a surface. You are choosing the boundaries of your imagination.

Dimensional Rigidity: When the Module Quietly Becomes the Designer

One of the most frustrating truths in façade execution is that most traditional materials come pre-decided.

They arrive with their own sizes, their own ratios, their own preferred directions, and their own rules about what can and cannot be cut from a sheet.

This means the façade you design must often accommodate the material rather than the material accommodating the façade.

A 1200 by 2400 sheet sounds harmless until you realize your façade demands a grid that needs 1375 by 2530 modules. You adjust the grid to fit the sheet. You shift the joints to match the layout. You reduce the reveal depth to suit what the material manufacturer can provide.

These changes look harmless in the early stages, but they have a cumulative effect on the purity of your idea.

The joint lines that felt intentional start feeling slightly off. The proportions soften. The repetition changes character. The final façade retains the outline of your vision but loses the crispness that made it powerful.

Weather-Driven Degradation: Where the Façade Begins Aaging Faster Than the Building

India's climate presents one of the most demanding environments for façade materials. High UV exposure, unpredictable monsoons, dust-heavy winds, coastal salinity, temperature extremes, and continuous thermal expansion and contraction create conditions that challenge material performance over time.

These forces often reveal material behaviour that is not immediately apparent at the design or installation stage.

- **HPL gradually fades and loses colour** stability when exposed to prolonged direct sunlight.
- **ACP begins to show surface deformation and oil-canning effects** as substructures expand and contract under thermal stress.
- **Stone loses colour uniformity and absorbs moisture unevenly,** leading to staining and patchy ageing across elevations.
- **Terracotta develops visible discoloration over time** due to variations in firing, moisture exposure, and environmental deposits.
- **Glass experiences thermal stress, staining,** and sealant deterioration, particularly in high-exposure conditions.
- **GRC develops micro-cracks** that can propagate gradually as thermal movement and structural stresses accumulate.
- **Slim tiles, while visually refined, are sensitive to substrate movement** and installation quality, often showing cracking, debonding, or edge damage when subjected to thermal cycling and moisture ingress.
- **WPC louvers can experience colour fading, surface chalking**, and dimensional movement over

time, especially under continuous UV exposure and fluctuating temperatures.

- **IPE and other dense hardwoods**, including Brazilian wood species, are highly durable but still respond to Indian climatic conditions through colour change, surface weathering, and dimensional movement if not detailed, treated, and maintained appropriately.

None of these behaviours is immediately visible on the day of installation.

This is why they are often underestimated during material selection. Five years later, however, the façade tells a different story. The building begins to age unevenly, and the first element the client notices is the façade. The architect, unfortunately, becomes the easiest target for blame, even though the material was never designed to remain visually unchanged under such conditions.

Fixing System Visibility: The Slow Erosion of Elegance

Clean lines, concealed joints, and a quiet aesthetic signature are essential to contemporary façade expression.

Traditional materials struggle to support this level of subtlety because their fixing systems depend heavily on visible components.

Screws, rivets, clamps, adhesives, and structural supports begin to reveal themselves through shadows, angles, gaps, or slight protrusions. The façade starts looking manufactured rather than crafted. Even when the execution team does its best, the constraints of the material make it nearly impossible to hide every fixing detail.

The façade ends up looking technical rather than architectural.

The purity of the original idea gives way to practicality, and the moment this happens, the architect feels the loss immediately. It is the kind of visual disruption only the creator notices at first, but eventually everyone does.

Inconsistent Performance Across Elevations: The Façade Feels Different From Each Side

A façade is rarely a single surface. Each orientation behaves differently. Traditional materials are highly sensitive to orientation, which means your carefully designed façade rarely ages uniformly.

- The east façade absorbs morning moisture.
- The west façade receives harsh direct sun.
- The south façade feels wind pressure differently.
- The north façade often collects dust and pollution.

When materials react differently to the environment, the façade begins developing multiple personalities.

Shade variations appear. Joints shift differently. Expansion behaves unpredictably. The building begins to lose its cohesive identity, even if the design was meant to feel unified.

Most architects have seen this happen on at least one project, even if no one pointed out the cause.

Substructure Sensitivity: When the Material Exposes Every Hidden Mistake

This is the limitation architects struggle with the most across façade systems. Most façade materials, including metal façades, depend heavily on reasonably accurate

RCC conditions. They require exact alignments, straight beams, proper bracket spacing, and consistent tolerances. Unfortunately, real construction rarely offers this level of perfection.

When the structure is off by even a few millimeters, the façade displays the mistake openly.

Joints stop aligning. Panel edges behave unpredictably. Surfaces twist. Shadows break rhythm. Even the slightest deviation in plumb or level becomes an aesthetic disruption.

You designed a façade with perfection in mind.

In metal façades, however, finish choices, joint strategies, and detailing depth offer greater flexibility to visually manage and absorb minor structural deviations.

Key Takeaways

- Traditional façade materials carry predictable limitations that emerge during execution. These universal failures weaken design intent long before the façade is installed.
- The limitations are systemic and inherent, not the result of poor architectural decision-making.

Recognising these boundaries helps you choose materials that support rather than restrict your vision.

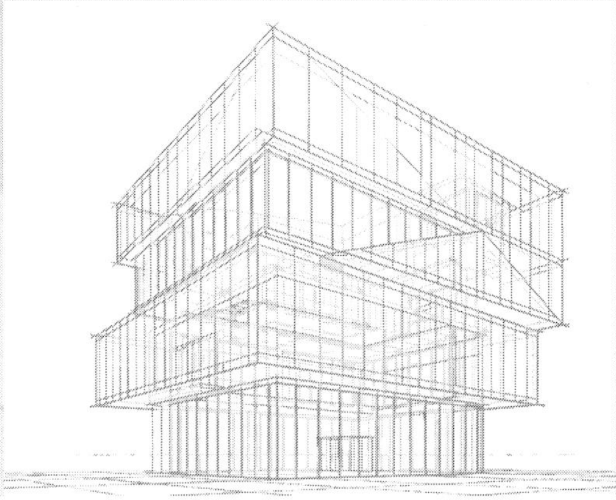

PART II
UNDERSTANDING METAL FAÇADES

Chapter 4

What Changes When the Façade Is Metal

There is a moment in every architect's career when you realise that your ideas have outgrown the materials you have been working with.

- You feel it the day your form wants to twist slightly, but the material wants to stay flat.
- You feel it the moment your intuition tells you a façade needs depth, only for the engineering team to remind you that the surface cannot hold it.
- You feel it when your design vocabulary begins shifting toward sculptural, layered, precise expressions that demand far more than a panel stuck to a wall.

At some point, your imagination simply becomes too big for most façade materials.

This is where metal enters the story.

Metal is not the future because it is trendy or because the world suddenly discovered aluminium. Metal is the future because it is the only façade material whose behaviour aligns with the way contemporary architects think today. The world has moved beyond flat façades, repetitive grids, and purely functional skins. Architecture has shifted toward identity, movement, emotion, light, and story.

Façades are no longer backgrounds. They are signatures.

And metal is the only medium that treats architecture like a signature rather than a surface.

The World is Moving from Two Dimensions to Three

For decades, façades behaved as if they lived in two dimensions.

You could push and pull slightly, but the canvas was mostly flat.

The language was panel-based.

Expression stayed inside a limited vocabulary.

But modern architecture does not think in two dimensions anymore. Forms twist. Edges taper. Volumes dissolve. Surfaces want to breathe. Architects are thinking like sculptors, choreographers, and even composers.

The façade is not a shell. It is the emotional introduction to a building.

Metal is the only façade material that naturally accepts this evolution. Not reluctantly, but enthusiastically.

Metal does not tell you what to avoid.

Metal tells you what else you can try.

- It lets surfaces curve.
- It lets volumes shift.
- It lets perforated patterns control light with precision.
- It lets layers float over each other without losing structural clarity.
- It lets architects finally design in three dimensions without apology.

This is not about abandoning panels.

This is about graduating from them.

Metal Behaves Like a Design Medium, Not a Sheet

When you begin working with metal, a quiet shift happens.

You stop seeing it as a product and start recognising it as a medium. Metal is expressive. Metal is responsive. Metal is obedient when you want it to be and rebellious in creative ways when you push it further.

Metal lets you design with the confidence that the form you imagined is the form you will receive. It respects angles. It respects curves. It respects joints. It respects depth. It respects the honesty of your lines in a way that few materials ever can.

Architects often speak about metal the way artists speak about materials. There is a kind of relief in not having to negotiate with your own imagination.

Metal adapts to complexity instead of avoiding it

The more complex your idea, the more excited metal becomes. It does not complain when you introduce tapering geometries or subtle curvature. It does not panic when you design a façade that changes depth across floors. It does not protest when you want a parametric rhythm that shifts based on light.

Metal thrives on complexity because metal does not simply exist in a finished form.

- It is engineered.
- It is shaped.
- It is interpreted.
- It is composed.

And that engineering process gives you a level of control that architects rarely experience with any other façade medium.

When you design with metal, you are not designing a façade.

You are designing a system.

- You control the folds.
- You control the stiffness.
- You control the thickness.
- You control the coating.
- You control the reflectivity.
- You control the perforation logic.
- You control how it behaves with light.
- You control how it expresses structure.
- You control how it absorbs tolerances.

- You control how it speaks to the surroundings.

Architects generally gain more authorship over a façade when working with metal than with any other material. And that authorship is intoxicating.

Metal unlocks the precision architects crave

There is a moment when you look at a façade and feel an immediate sense of satisfaction. Even before analysing the design, you know something is right. The shadows align. The joints behave silently. The geometry holds its intention. The surface feels confident. The entire façade appears composed rather than assembled.

This clarity happens when precision meets purpose. And metal excels at precision.

Metal allows you to pursue a design language defined by crispness, alignment, and disciplined expression. When your drawings call for a 12 millimeter reveal, metal

delivers 12. When your façade needs a consistent shadow line, metal maintains it. When your grid depends on accuracy for its rhythm, metal follows your command each time.

Architecture is often a negotiation.

Metal is one of the few materials that negotiates in your favour.

The world's aesthetic direction already favors metal

Look around at the most admired buildings of the last decade.

You will notice a pattern.

The façades that feel contemporary, sculptural, intelligent, and timeless almost always use metal.

This is not accidental.

Global architectural language has changed.

We are seeing a shift toward forms that want to:

Float... Twist... Fold... Hover... Peel... Dissolve... Wrap... Filter light... Behave dynamically throughout the day

Metal is the only façade medium that can interpret all these gestures without losing structural integrity or expressive control.

This is why architects in London, Dubai, Singapore, Copenhagen, Melbourne, and Seoul are not just choosing metal. They are depending on it.

Metal is not catching up with the world.

Metal is the reason the world has moved ahead.

Metal supports hybrid façades beautifully

Contemporary façades rarely rely on one material. Architects mix. They fuse. They layer. They integrate experiences into the surface itself.

Metal is the only façade material that effortlessly collaborates with others.

- It harmonises with glass.
- It anchors stone.
- It frames terracotta.
- It complements concrete.
- It integrates lighting with the façade.
- It softens transitions.
- It sharpens identities.

Metal is the glue that makes hybrid façades feel intentional instead of chaotic. It becomes the unifying grammar of the elevation.

In a world where architectural storytelling is deeply layered, metal provides the thread that weaves those layers into a meaningful whole.

Metal introduces a new structural intelligence to façades

When you design with metal, you are not just designing the skin.

You are designing the intelligence behind the skin.

Metal systems allow you to define substructure logic, panel behaviour, fold geometry, stiffness, load transfer, shadow effect, drainage, and depth variation. This is an extraordinary level of control for architects. It gives you the ability to direct not just what the façade looks like, but how it behaves.

In traditional façade systems, the material dictates the system.

In metal façades, the architect dictates the system.

That is the subtle but powerful shift.

Metal is the only façade material compatible with the future of lighting

Architecture today is incomplete without lighting identity.

Every building speaks twice.

Once in daylight.

Once at night.

Metal is the most lighting-friendly façade medium in existence. It can glow. It can filter. It can silhouette. It can reflect. It can refract. It can soften. It can dramatise. It can create patterns of light that feel like movement, not illumination.

Perforated metal, especially, is a playground for lighting designers. It allows architects to script the night identity of a building with control, nuance, and imagination.

Metal does not just support lighting.

Metal transforms it.

Metal is the architect's return to creative power

At some point in your career, you may have felt that your façade was being redesigned by everyone except you.

Structural shifts force compromises. Modules force grid changes. Tolerances force joint deviations. Fixing systems forces visual concessions. Vendors force simplifications.

Metal reverses that dynamic.

With metal, you define the language.

Metal follows your grammar.

You write the rules.

Metal expresses them consistently.

You know exactly how your façade will behave even before the first panel is made. There is a confidence in that knowledge that architects deeply appreciate because it gives you something rare in the world of construction.

Control.

MetaMask's Relationship with Metal is Different

To some people, metal is a sheet.

To MetaMask, metal is a medium of design intelligence.

At MetaMask, we do not simply manufacture panels.

We engineer experiences.

We interpret your drawings with an understanding of form, behaviour, tolerance, and alignment.

We treat metal the way a printer treats ink.

Not as a component, but as the language of the outcome.

> "Metal is one of the few façade materials that lets architects design with fewer compromises. It expands the vision instead of forcing it to be trimmed."
>
> **- Ankur Hora, Founder of MetaMask**

This is not a slogan.

It is the truth that every architect feels once they experience a well-executed metal façade.

Metal does not protect itself.

MetaMask protects the metal that protects your design.

Why This Chapter Matters

By the end of Part I, you understood the limitations architects face when they want their designs to perform in the real world.

Part II is about introducing you to a new world where your

ideas no longer need to shrink to fit material limitations.

Metal is not a substitute.

Metal is a new category.

A category built for architects whose imagination does not stay inside the lines.

In the next chapter, you will see just how far metal can take your design. And why most of the forms you have admired in global architecture were not accidents. They were creations that metal allowed to exist.

Metal is not the future.

Metal is the present that architects are finally ready to claim.

Key Takeaways

- Metal is the first façade medium that treats architecture as a three-dimensional expression rather than a two-dimensional covering.
- It behaves like a design medium, not a sheet, and responds to complexity with clarity.
- Metal gives architects authorship, precision, lighting compatibility, and hybrid integration power.
- It aligns with the global direction of sculptural, minimalistic, parametric, and identity-driven architecture.

With the right engineering partner, metal becomes the material that expands your creativity instead of restricting it.

Chapter 5

Design Possibilities You Cannot Achieve with Anything Else

Every architect remembers the moment a design idea grows bigger than the material meant to express it. It might happen when the form begins to undulate instead of staying flat. Or when the façade demands a gesture instead of a grid. Or when your mind drifts toward a sculptural move that cannot be flattened into a panel.

Most façade materials force you to scale back that instinct.

Metal encourages you to explore it.

Metal is the only façade medium that expands your vocabulary instead of shrinking it.

It behaves like something alive. It bends, flows, accepts complexity, translates intention, and remains obedient to the precision you need. It allows architecture to feel like choreography instead of coverage.

This chapter explores the design territories that **only metal** allows you to access. Not enhancements. Not alternatives. Entire possibilities that do not exist in any other system.

Design Becomes Sculpture, Not Surface

There is a whole universe of design where the façade behaves like a sculpture instead of a surface.

Metal is the only material that makes this universe real rather than theoretical.

- You can twist a plane like fabric held in motion.
- You can fold it sharply without weakening the form.
- You can push and pull volumes like a malleable shell.
- You can taper edges so cleanly that the shadow becomes part of the design.
- You can create forms that carry movement without compromising structure.

Architects often speak about metal with a sense of relief.

It lets you design the way you think, not the way a material forces you to think.

Curves and organic forms finally become realistic

Curvature is a natural state for metal.

It bends predictably.

It holds strength while curved.

It accepts smooth radii and tight bends.

It repeats complex curves with perfect consistency when engineered correctly. **This unlocks:**

Soft sweeping shells... Compound curves... Curved fins... Transition surfaces that shift from flat to curved... Vertical or horizontal bending logic... Continuous ribbons of form.

Curves used to be rare moments in Indian façades.

With metal, they can become everyday design tools.

Depth becomes an architectural language

Depth is one of architecture's most expressive tools. Most materials treat depth as a burden. Metal treats depth as a playground.

You can create:

- Floating planes
- Deep fins
- Layered screens
- Shadow pockets
- Ribs and boxes
- Cantilevered projections
- Subtle recesses that behave like sculpted voids

Metal maintains elegance even when the façade extends outward.

- It does not distort.
- It does not stretch.
- It does not feel heavy.

Depth stops being an engineering challenge and starts becoming a design strategy.

Perforations: A Language that Belongs Only to Metal

Perforated metal is a category of design that has no real equivalent. It turns metal into a breathing, glowing, filtering skin.

Perforations allow you to design four things at once:

1. **Transparency control**

   You can decide exactly how much the façade reveals or hides.

2. **Airflow and ventilation**

   Without adding grills or exposed elements.

3. **Dynamic shadow patterns**

   The sun becomes part of the design.

4. **Night identity**

   Backlighting transforms the façade into a luminous experience.

Perforations let architects script movement through light, shadow, and visibility. You are not applying ornament.

You are designing behaviour.

Where These Design Possibilities Come Alive

These design possibilities are not theoretical.

They are already shaping architecture across multiple layers of the built environment.

Applications

Metal design strategies described in this chapter are increasingly used in:

- Building façades and envelopes
- Feature façades and signature elevations
- Interior and exterior screens
- Ceiling planes and soffits
- Sun-shading systems and second skins
- Transition zones, atriums, and semi-open spaces

Project types

Architects are applying these expressions across:

- Jewellery stores and luxury retail environments
- Commercial buildings and office campuses
- Industrial facilities and factories seeking a refined identity

- Shopping malls and mixed-use developments
- Cultural buildings, auditoriums, and public institutions
- Stadiums, arenas, and large-format public infrastructure

What connects all these projects is not scale or budget.

It is the need for a façade system that can express identity, control environment, and carry design intent without compromise.

Parametric Geometry Becomes Practical

Parametric façades often die between software and site.

Metal bridges that gap.

Parametric design depends on:

Controlled variation... repetitive modules... adaptable geometry... precise alignment... predictable structural behaviour.

Metal excels on all fronts.

- It can repeat complex modules without distortion.
- It can vary panel sizes without breaking alignment.
- It can support twisting geometries with engineered stiffness.
- It can handle gradient patterns across large surfaces.

The world's most successful parametric façades are metal for a reason. The material keeps up with the mathematics.

The Architect Regains Authorship

Most façade materials control you.

Metal lets you control them.

When you work with metal, you design the folds, the stiffness, the behaviour, the transitions, the edges, the shadow logic, the joints, and the system behind the skin.

The façade becomes a medium of authorship rather than a surface of negotiation.

> "Metal allows the architect to translate imagination into physical precision without losing the emotion of the idea"
>
> **- Ankur Hora, Founder of MetaMask**

This is why metal does not replace anything.

It elevates everything.

Key Takeaways

- Working with metal allows façades to explore sculptural form, fluid geometry, and controlled depth with greater reliability.
- Metal systems enable precise control over perforation, transparency, and light-based expression when detailed correctly.
- Parametric design becomes more practical to execute when the material system can repeat, adapt, and align consistently.

- Metal façades can be designed to act as environmental moderators, supporting airflow, privacy, and climatic response.
- When integrated thoughtfully, metal helps unify hybrid façades and retain clarity of architectural intent through execution.

Chapter 6

The 9 Hidden Sutras to Know Before Choosing Metal Façades

Every architect knows the familiar heartbreak of watching a brilliant façade design lose its clarity once it enters the real world. The drawings look promising. The concept feels aligned. The forms behave beautifully in the model. Yet something happens between intention and installation. Panels shift. Joints misbehave. Brackets appear where they should not. Fixings dictate aesthetics. Curves deform. Lighting becomes complicated. The purity of the design dissolves into a series of compromises that feel almost personal.

This collapse happens because metal façades follow their own internal logic. It is a logic that most architects were never taught, and that vendors rarely explain. When ignored, the façade becomes unpredictable. When understood, the façade becomes the most controllable and expressive medium in contemporary architecture.

MetaMask refers to this internal logic as the Nine Hidden Sutras.

- They are not mystical ideas, nor are they complex engineering theories meant only for specialists.
- They are the fundamental truths governing how metal behaves, how it must be detailed, how it interacts with geometry and light, and how it ultimately translates the architect's vision into reality.

Architects who understand these sutras work with metal the way a sculptor works with clay, confidently and without hesitation. Architects who do not understand them spend months correcting mistakes that should never have happened.

These sutras are revealed here with complete transparency so that your designs no longer depend on interpretation or luck. Once you master them, you will gain a level of control over your façades that most professionals never experience in their entire careers.

SUTRA 1

Form Must Follow Engineering Logic

A metal façade may look like an artistic surface, but it behaves like a structural object. Before a line is drawn, the architect must understand how metal prefers to move, how it prefers to bend, how it distributes loads, and how it responds to shape. Many façade failures begin not at the fabrication stage but at the moment of conceptualisation, when a beautiful form is imagined without considering the forces that will eventually act on it.

Every curve carries a natural behaviour. Every fold introduces stiffness. Every change in depth alters structural stress. Every area of openness, especially in perforated panels, affects how the panel will hold its shape. Metal is capable of extraordinary forms, but those forms must grow out of an understanding of what the material wants to do. When the engineering logic of the façade is respected from the outset, the design remains stable and elegant throughout execution. When it is ignored, the façade begins to resist the architect in subtle but persistent ways.

- This sutra teaches that beauty must be built on logic.
- A façade that respects the laws of its material expresses design with effortless confidence.

SUTRA 2

Depth Must Be Decided Before the Concept Freezes

Depth is one of the most powerful tools available to an architect working with metal. It shapes shadow, reinforces structure, influences the substructure layout, defines the reading of the form, and plays a vital role in lighting integration. Yet depth is surprisingly one of the least resolved aspects of conceptual design.

When depth is left undecided, the façade has no spine. As the design progresses, the unresolved depth begins creating inconsistencies. Brackets are forced into larger

projections than the design intended. Panels no longer align in the rhythm the architect wanted. Joints lose clarity. Lighting recesses becomes awkward rather than elegant. The façade starts drifting away from the original intention, even if the drawings technically remain the same.

Depth must be fixed early. A façade that knows its depth from the beginning becomes predictable and consistent. A façade that experiments with depth too late becomes unstable. Once depth is frozen at the concept stage, every subsequent layer of engineering and fabrication behaves with complete clarity.

- Depth is not decoration.
- Depth is structure. And in metal, structure is visual language.

SUTRA 3

The Substructure Decides the Fate of the Façade

Every architect has faced a façade that looked beautiful on paper but fell apart on site. The cause is almost always the same. The substructure was not planned with the same intention as the outer skin.

Panels are only the visible body of the façade. The soul of the façade is the substructure that holds it. It is the substructure that ensures joints stay straight, that alignment remains true, that panels do not vibrate, that tolerances are absorbed gracefully, and that the façade maintains its form regardless of environmental forces. A poorly planned substructure forces the panels to compensate for structural weakness, leading to misalignment, waviness, and a general lack of precision.

A well-planned substructure is not merely a set of aluminium or steel members. It is an invisible architecture designed with intention. It follows the logic of the façade's geometry, supports the depth and curvature, aligns with joint rhythms, anticipates thermal movement, and creates a stable foundation for the final expression.

➢ If you want the façade to look refined, begin by refining the substructure.

SUTRA 4

Every Curve Has a Minimum Radius

Metal welcomes curves, but only when they are introduced with an understanding of the material's temperament. Every curve, no matter how gentle or dramatic, has a natural minimum radius that depends on the alloy, the thickness, the temper, and the finishing process. When an architect designs a curve without knowing the minimum radius, the form may look perfect on the drawing, but behave unpredictably during fabrication.

If the curvature is too tight for the material to handle, the panel will express its discomfort. Coatings may develop microfractures. Edges may show stress marks. Panels may spring back slightly, refusing to hold the exact radius drawn in the model. The larger the panel, the more pronounced these reactions become.

But when an architect designs within the natural radius limits of the material, metal behaves with elegance. It bends smoothly, holds its form consistently, and allows repetition without variation. The façade becomes a sequence of fluid gestures rather than a collection of forced movements.

- Curves succeed when they respect the boundaries of the material.
- The moment the architect learns these boundaries, curved façades become a joy rather than a challenge.

SUTRA 5

Perforations Are a Structural Decision, Not a Decoration

Perforated metal façades are among the most visually captivating elements in contemporary design. They create dynamic shadows, allow light to pass through like a woven fabric, and give the building a sense of lightness and depth. Yet perforations are often misunderstood as purely decorative decisions.

The reality is far more complex. Every perforation changes how the panel behaves structurally. As holes are introduced, stiffness reduces. Weight changes. The panel's ability to resist wind pressure shifts. The structural demands on the substructure evolve. The edges of the panel become more sensitive. Even the finishing process behaves differently on perforated surfaces.

To design perforations responsibly, the architect must consider the relationship between open area and stiffness, the distribution of the pattern, the distance of perforations from edges, and the functional purpose behind transparency. When this understanding is present, perforated façades become masterpieces of both aesthetics and engineering. When absent, they become panels that vibrate, warp, or distort long after installation.

- Perforation is not surface art.
- Perforation is a structural sculpture.

SUTRA 6

Joint Logic Must Be Decided Before the Panel Is Ever Drawn

Joints are the grammar of a façade. They define rhythm, scale, alignment, transitions, and the overall visual coherence of the building. Yet joints are often treated as secondary details, decided after the paneling is conceptualised. Metal façades cannot be designed this way.

The joint strategy must come first. The size of the reveal, the depth of the shadow, the alignment with the building grid, the transition at corners, and the continuity across levels must all be determined before a single panel shape is created. Once the joint logic is clear, the panel modules reveal themselves naturally. When joints are an afterthought, the façade feels noisy and disjointed, as if the panels were placed independently rather than composed intentionally.

- Great façades are not defined by their panels.
- They are defined by the space between the panels.

SUTRA 7

Thermal Expansion Must Be Designed, Not Tolerated

Metal has a living quality. It expands in heat and contracts in cold. These movements are natural and consistent. Yet architects often treat thermal expansion as an inconvenience rather than a design factor. When ignored, thermal expansion manifests later as bulging panels, popped fixings, cracked joints, misaligned corners, or audible noises as the panels struggle to resist movement.

A metal façade succeeds only when thermal movement is respected. This means allowing panels to float where necessary, allowing the substructure to accommodate temperature shifts, and designing joints that absorb rather than resist expansion. When temperature variation becomes part of the design rather than an afterthought, the façade behaves with quiet confidence, regardless of weather.

- Metal is not rigid. Its beauty lies in its flexibility.
- And the architect's understanding of this flexibility determines the long-term performance of the façade.

SUTRA 8

Fixing Points Are Design Decisions, Not Site Decisions

In many projects, fixing points are left for the fabricator

or site team to interpret. This is one of the most common reasons metal façades fail aesthetically. Fixings decide how flat the panel stays, how it aligns with adjacent panels, how it handles wind pressure, how it behaves during temperature changes, and how long it maintains structural integrity.

Fixings must be drawn, not assumed. The number of fixings, their exact positions, their interaction with the substructure, the material used, the strategy for concealment, and their accessibility for maintenance must be planned with intention.

- The moment the site team is allowed to make fixing decisions, the architecture loses its authorship.
- When fixings are treated as design rather than improvisation, the façade reads as a single continuous thought rather than a collection of installed parts.

SUTRA 9

Mockups Are the Truth, Drawings Are Theory

No façade becomes real until the mockup reveals its truth. Drawings are interpretations. Renders are aspirations. Mockups are reality.

A full-scale mockup shows the actual behaviour of joints, the authenticity of the shadow lines, the performance of the coating, the crispness of bends, the uniformity of perforations, the integration of lighting, and the overall visual language that the façade will express. It exposes flaws long before they become costly mistakes. It allows the architect to refine the final expression with complete confidence.

- Architects who insist on mockups create façades that look like their drawings. Architects who skip mockups create façades that resemble approximations.
- Mockups are not an extra step. They are the final drawings.

"A metal façade succeeds only when the architect and the engineer agree on the rules of the material. These sutras are not secrets. They are the discipline behind beauty."

- Ankur Hora, Founder of MetaMask

KEY TAKEAWAYS

Metal façades succeed when the architect understands the underlying rules that govern form, depth, curvature, perforation, joints, thermal behaviour, fixings, and substructure design.

The Nine Hidden Sutras transform metal from a potentially unpredictable material into one that behaves with precision and reliability.

When these sutras are applied from the concept stage onward, the façade's outcome becomes controlled, intentional, and aesthetically consistent. Knowledge of these sutras protects the architect's design intent from being diluted by vendor improvisation or site limitations.

Mastering these principles allows your façade to look exactly as it was imagined, rather than as an approximation formed through compromises.

PART III
WHERE FAÇADES FAIL AND HOW TO PREVENT IT

Chapter 7

The Planning Stage Blind Spots

The planning stage is the place where architects hold the most power and simultaneously lose the most control. All the creativity of the concept stage, all the technical intelligence of the engineering stage, and all the craftsmanship of the execution stage depend on the decisions made here. Poor planning does not simply lead to delays. It leads to façades that feel slightly "off," façades that look acceptable from a distance but frustrating up close, façades that make architects feel the work no longer reflects their intention.

To understand why planning determines everything, you must recognise a simple truth: a façade is not a product. It is a system. And like every system, it succeeds or fails based on how clearly its rules are set at the beginning.

In this chapter, we explore the most consistent and costly planning-stage mistakes architects encounter. These mistakes are universal. They appear in residential towers, commercial complexes, hospitality projects, industrial facades, and even high-end boutiques. They do not discriminate by budget or brand. They occur because the industry has normalised certain assumptions about façades that do not align with how façades actually behave.

Once you understand these mistakes, you will never approach façade planning the same way again. They will become invisible red flags that reveal themselves instantly in meetings, drawings, and client discussions. They will save your design from dilution, your site from chaos, and your reputation from blame that was never yours to begin with.

THE FIRST BLIND SPOT

Treating the Façade Like a Skin Instead of a System

Façades are often approached as if they were the building's clothing. Something applied after the real design work is done. Something decorative. Something adjustable. Something that can be modified later. This is one of the most dangerous assumptions in architecture.

A façade is a system woven deeply into the structural grid, the MEP spine, the lighting strategy, and the ventilation requirements of a building. When the façade is treated like a skin, it is pushed to the end of the planning conversation. That is usually where trouble begins.

A façade that is treated as an afterthought will keep demanding revisions. The client will keep changing their preferences because nothing feels final. The structural team will keep encountering conflicts because the façade was not accounted for. The MEP team will keep placing ducts, conduits, and openings wherever they find convenient. The site team will keep improvising solutions because no one knows what the façade needs to protect or conceal.

A façade becomes stable only when it is considered the building's external architecture, not its external decoration.

The planning stage is where this awareness must be established. When the façade is integrated into the earliest architectural and engineering discussions, every later decision aligns with it naturally.

THE SECOND BLIND SPOT

Limited Client Awareness at an Early Stage of Façade Planning

Façades are rarely chosen purely on logic.

They are experienced visually, emotionally, and symbolically. Clients imagine how a building will be perceived long before they understand what a façade decision affects beneath the surface.

At early stages, façade discussions often revolve around appearance. Colours, textures, and visual impact take centre stage, while the deeper implications of façade choices remain abstract. Budgets, timelines, coordination requirements, and system dependencies usually enter the conversation much later.

When façade decisions are made before these implications are fully visible, the façade begins to absorb shifting priorities.

- Aesthetic preferences evolve. Functional requirements surface. Expectations change. What started as a visual choice slowly becomes a moving target.
- Material switches trigger structural recalibration.
- Thickness changes affect edge conditions.
- Perforation decisions influence airflow, brackets, and services.
- Each adjustment ripples quietly through structure, MEP coordination, detailing, and installation sequencing.

The challenge here is not communication.

It is timing.

When clarity arrives late, changes feel inevitable.

When clarity arrives early, stability follows naturally.

Early visibility into what façade decisions unlock—and what they constrain—creates alignment. Choices become deliberate. Commitments come sooner. The planning stage stabilises because fewer assumptions are left unresolved.

When this alignment exists, façade decisions stop drifting.

And when façade decisions stop drifting, the rest of the project finds its footing.

THE THIRD BLIND SPOT

Structural Grid and Façade Intent Not Aligned

Nothing compromises a façade faster than a structural grid that does not align with façade intent. Columns positioned without considering elevation logic often lead to

bracket projections, exposed fixings, misaligned joints, and residual spaces that weaken the clarity of the overall façade.

At the planning stage, structural logic and façade intent are often developed in parallel, guided by different priorities. Structural systems respond to load paths and efficiency. Façade systems respond to form, rhythm, and visual continuity. When these logics are aligned early, the elevation resolves with ease. When they evolve independently, the façade absorbs the friction between them.

Many façade distortions trace back to moments when structural decisions were finalised before façade alignment requirements were fully visible.

Clean elevations on the outside frequently rely on structural grids that have been intentionally coordinated from the inside. When this coordination happens early, the façade reads as intentional. When it happens late, compromise becomes unavoidable.

THE FOURTH BLIND SPOT

Overlooking Openings and Functional Penetrations

Every building requires exhaust vents, shaft openings, fresh air intakes, AC penetrations, and multiple service pathways to pass through the façade. When these requirements surface late in the process, they tend to appear reactively during execution. Panels are cut on site. Substructures are adjusted. Grills and covers are added as afterthoughts. Visual coherence begins to break down.

Openings are not interruptions. They are part of the façade system. When they are anticipated early, they can be resolved with geometry, rhythm, and alignment. Their presence feels intentional rather than imposed. Integration replaces patchwork.

Challenges arise when functional requirements become visible only after façade systems are already defined. In such cases, the façade is forced to absorb decisions it was never designed to accommodate. What follows is not poor design, but late coordination.

Façades that read clean and composed often do so because functional penetrations were accounted for from the beginning. When visibility comes early, resolution feels effortless. When it comes late, compromise becomes unavoidable.

THE FIFTH BLIND SPOT

MEP Integration Left to the Last Minute

MEP systems and façade systems often evolve on parallel tracks during early planning. Each responds to different functional priorities, and their points of intersection are not always fully visible at the outset. When these intersections surface late, they tend to appear during execution rather than design.

At that stage, adjustments happen on site. Penetrations are introduced reactively. Cable trays, lighting lines, HVAC ducts, and access points are accommodated through improvisation. This is rarely intentional, and it almost always places stress on the façade system.

Improvisation is the enemy of façade integrity.

Façades perform best when space for services is anticipated early. When penetrations align with joint lines, when ducts are absorbed into depth, when wiring is concealed within recesses, and when access requirements are resolved as part of the form, the relationship between architecture and services feels seamless.

When MEP integration is addressed alongside façade design, the elevation remains composed, execution becomes calmer, and the final outcome reads as deliberate rather than corrected.

THE SIXTH BLIND SPOT

Late Lighting Planning

Lighting plays a defining role in how a façade is perceived. It shapes shadow, mood, identity, and the way a building is read after dark. Because of this, lighting cannot function as a secondary layer added once the façade is complete. It must be resolved as part of the façade system itself.

When lighting considerations surface late in the process, they are forced to adapt to decisions already made. Fixtures begin to compete with geometry. Brackets and wiring become visible. Elements that should disappear start asserting themselves. Visual clarity gives way to clutter.

Lighting performs best when it is anticipated early. When folds, recesses, joints, and edges are shaped with illumination in mind, light feels embedded rather than applied. The façade develops a nighttime presence that aligns naturally with its daytime form. The building reads as one continuous idea rather than two separate expressions.

In metal façades especially, lighting has the ability to amplify depth, articulation, and identity. For this potential to be realised, lighting integration must be addressed as a core planning consideration, not as a late-stage addition.

THE SEVENTH BLIND SPOT

Installing the Parapet Before Understanding the Façade

Parapets are often executed early in the project because they appear structurally straightforward. Yet the parapet interacts directly with the façade. Its height, thickness, cap detail, and alignment influence the paneling, the corner transitions, the drainage, and the top edge expression of the façade.

When the parapet is installed before the façade intent is clear, architects lose valuable flexibility. The façade becomes forced to work around a rigid top boundary, resulting in misalignment, awkward flashing details, visible sealants, or unnecessary steps between panels and parapet surfaces.

A façade's top line is its conclusion. It must be designed, not inherited.

THE EIGHTH BLIND SPOT

Underestimating Offsets and Substructure Margins

Offsets are the silent killers of façade precision. They appear harmless in drawings and look negligible in early discussions. But every offset shifts the substructure. Every shift changes bracket lengths. Every bracket length alters panel alignment. Every alignment shift affects joint straightness. And every joint deviation affects the entire reading of the façade.

Offsets must be calculated carefully in the planning stage. They must consider insulation, waterproofing, tolerances, panel depth, joint logic, bracket distances, and site

conditions. If offsets are planned vaguely, the façade begins accumulating micro errors that eventually become macro distractions.

Architects who master offsets control the façade's geometry with absolute clarity.

THE NINTH BLIND SPOT

Mixing Products Without Understanding Their Margins

Façades are rarely composed of a single material. More often, they bring together metal, glass, stone, terracotta, and other systems into a unified envelope. Each of these materials carries its own thickness, tolerance range, installation method, and visual weight. When these characteristics are not resolved together early, junctions begin to feel forced, transitions appear abrupt, and continuity at corners becomes difficult to maintain.

Material fusion is most successful when margin behaviour is visible at the pre-design stage. Differences in thickness, fixing depth, movement allowance, and joint logic need to be reconciled before systems are locked. When these relationships remain unresolved, the façade absorbs the mismatch during execution.

Façades that read as a single composition often do so because material margins were aligned early. Transitions feel intentional. Junctions remain calm.

The envelope holds together visually and technically. When margin behaviour becomes visible late, the façade risks reading as an assembly of parts rather than a coherent whole.

THE TENTH BLIND SPOT

Ignoring Sequence of Work and Timeline Dependencies

Façade installation does not happen in isolation. It sits within a tightly linked chain of activities that includes waterproofing, MEP routing, civil finishing, structural readiness, and multiple parallel site operations. The outcome of the façade is directly influenced by how these activities intersect over time.

When sequencing relationships are not clearly resolved early, the façade begins absorbing the impact of unrelated delays and accelerations. Work gets compressed.

Access windows shrink. Protective measures are removed prematurely. Elements that require precision are exposed to rushed conditions.

Effective sequencing brings clarity to when brackets are installed, when substructures are completed, when waterproofing interfaces are resolved, when MEP access is required, when lighting cables are introduced, and when panel installation can proceed without interference. When these dependencies are visible early, execution becomes smoother and less reactive.

Clear sequencing discipline helps protect the façade from unnecessary delays, site damage, and rework. More importantly, it allows the façade to be executed in conditions that respect its design intent rather than compromise it under pressure.

THE ELEVENTH BLIND SPOT

Not Freezing the Budget for the Façade at the Start

Budget fluidity is a façade of chaos. When the budget is not fixed in the planning stage, every façade decision becomes conditional. Materials change. Depth reduces. Perforations disappear. Lighting gets postponed. Substructure thickness gets compromised. The façade becomes a negotiation rather than an expression.

A façade budget must be frozen early.

It must be understood as an essential architectural investment, not a luxury. Once the budget is fixed, design clarity follows. Without it, the façade becomes the area where compromises accumulate.

THE TWELFTH BLIND SPOT

Lack of Awareness About Timelines and Process

Many architects enter façade planning with artistic clarity but uncertain process knowledge. This leads to unrealistic expectations, compressed schedules, and unnecessary stress on the site team. Understanding the timeline is essential: how long engineering requires, how long production takes, how long coating requires, how long logistics may delay, and how long installation will realistically need.

When architects understand these timelines, they create schedules that support quality. When they do not, the façade must be rushed. A rushed façade is the enemy of elegance.

"Façade behaviour is cumulative. What appears on site is the result of how multiple decisions interact across the project lifecycle."

- Ankur Hora, Founder of MetaMask

KEY TAKEAWAYS

- Every major façade failure begins in the planning stage, long before panels are fabricated.
- Treating the façade as a system rather than a skin protects the architect's design intent. Early alignment with structure, MEP, lighting, openings, product fusion, and sequence prevents 90 per cent of site issues.

- ➢ Educating clients early stabilises façade decisions and prevents repeated design changes.

A well-planned façade behaves smoothly during engineering and installation, while a poorly planned one collapses into improvisation.

Chapter 8

When Product Choice Limits Design Possibilities

If the planning stage establishes the direction of a façade, product selection determines how far that direction can actually be explored. Materials do not merely clothe architecture. They define what forms can be attempted, what geometries can be sustained, and how faithfully an idea can survive fabrication, handling, installation, and time.

At the point of product selection, many variables converge. Visual intent, conceptual narratives, client aspirations, market availability, cost structures, and supplier inputs all intersect at once. At this stage, not every behavioural implication of a material is fully visible. Many characteristics only reveal themselves later, when the façade is asked to perform at scale.

In metal façades, especially, product choice does not decide how the façade looks alone. It decides what the façade is allowed to do.

This chapter explores how certain product choices quietly restrict design possibilities, while others allow architectural intent to remain fluid, expressive, and controlled through execution.

Design Expression Versus Material Behaviour

Every metal product carries two identities.

One is visual.

The other is behavioural.

The visual identity is what appears in catalogues, samples, and reference images. The behavioural identity emerges only when the material is bent, folded, coated, perforated, transported, installed, and exposed to climate.

A panel that appears smooth at hand-sample scale may express surface distortion when produced at large sizes.

A finish that feels rich under controlled lighting may lose depth under natural daylight. A coating that looks uniform on a flat panel may behave differently when applied to perforations or complex geometry.

Design intent expands only when visual ambition and material behaviour align. When they do not, the façade begins to resist its own expression.

Successful product selection does not begin with appearance alone. It begins with understanding how a material behaves once it is asked to perform across an entire building.

Alloy Choice and the Range of Form

Not all aluminium behaves the same way.

Different alloys carry different levels of stiffness, form retention, and resistance to deformation.

Softer alloys may allow easier initial forming, but struggle to hold long, flat lines or crisp folds at scale. Stronger alloys retain alignment, resist warping, and maintain consistency under thermal movement and handling stress.

The alloy selected quietly defines:

- How sharp folds can remain
- How straight do the edges stay over time
- How evenly does light reflect across large surfaces

When the alloy supports the intended geometry, the façade behaves predictably. When it does not, the design must compensate downstream.

Alloy selection, therefore, directly influences which design possibilities remain viable and which ones quietly fall away.

Thickness as a Design Enabler

Panel thickness is not merely a structural parameter. It is a design variable.

Thickness governs wind behaviour, surface flatness, resistance to vibration, visual stability, and bending feasibility.

Thinner panels allow tighter curvature but may introduce undulation. Thicker panels offer rigidity but resist certain forms. Thickness interacts with grid spacing, depth, and substructure logic to either support or constrain the design.

Refined façades rarely appear refined because of finish alone. They appear refined because thickness was aligned with geometry, scale, and behavioural expectations.

When thickness supports form, the façade remains composed.

When it does not, refinement is lost regardless of surface treatment.

Coatings and the Limits of Visual Longevity

Coatings define far more than colour. They determine how a façade ages.

Powder coatings, anodising, PVDF systems, sublimation finishes, and speciality treatments each respond differently to UV exposure, heat, pollution, moisture, and cleaning cycles. Their performance depends not only on type, but on chemistry, thickness, application process, and surface preparation.

A coating selected without understanding its exposure conditions may age unevenly. Panels begin to diverge in appearance. Certain areas fade faster. Maintenance becomes complex. The façade loses coherence long before its structural life ends.

Coating selection shapes not just initial expression, but long-term visual stability. A façade designed to endure deserves a coating chosen with equal foresight.

Handling, Scratch Resistance, and Real-World Execution

Metal panels travel long distances before they reach the building. They pass through fabrication lines, coating facilities, transport vehicles, site handling, and installation sequences.

Some finishes conceal minor marks naturally. Others reveal every touch.

When handling behaviour and site realities are not aligned with finish selection, panels arrive with imperfections that cannot be corrected without visual compromise.

A façade should not depend on ideal conditions to look intentional. Product choice must account for how materials behave during the journey, not just at the destination.

Grid Logic and Module Behaviour

Every metal façade system has an optimal panel size and grid rhythm. Panels that exceed behavioural limits distort. Panels that are too small increase joints, cost, and visual noise.

Grid selection influences joint alignment, shadow rhythm, structural efficiency, material wastage, and site handling practicality.

When grid logic is aligned with material behaviour, the façade reads as calm and intentional. When it is not, misalignment and inconsistency emerge despite best efforts during installation.

Grid decisions quietly determine whether a façade feels disciplined or restless.

Product Fusion and Transitional Clarity

Metal rarely exists alone. It meets glass, stone, concrete, terracotta, and other systems across a façade.

Each material carries its own thickness, reflectivity, tolerance, thermal movement, and fixing logic.

Design possibilities remain intact only when these behaviours are reconciled early. When transitions are resolved late, junctions become forced, depths misalign, and visual continuity breaks down.

Successful fusion allows materials to complement rather than compete.

Outdoor Behaviour and Scale Reality

Materials behave differently outdoors than they do in controlled environments. Light intensity, viewing distance, reflection, and atmospheric conditions transform how finishes are perceived.

A colour that feels subtle indoors may feel overpowering outdoors. A sheen that appears elegant at close range may become distracting at scale.

Design possibilities remain accurate only when finishes are evaluated under real conditions, at real dimensions, and alongside adjacent materials.

Product choice does not merely support design intent.

It defines its boundaries.

When material behaviour, scale, exposure, and execution realities are understood early, design possibilities expand. Forms remain fluid. Expression remains controlled. Intent survives the journey from drawing to building.

This chapter is not about avoiding errors.

It is about recognising how the right product choices allow architecture to do more, not less.

"Metal façades reveal their strengths and limitations as they move from concept to construction."

- Ankur Hora, Founder of MetaMask

KEY TAKEAWAYS

- Product choice defines which design possibilities remain viable at scale.
- Alloy, thickness, coating behaviour, and grid logic directly influence form, stability, and longevity.
- Visual samples alone cannot predict real-world performance.
- The most effective façades emerge when material behaviour and architectural intent are aligned early.

Design expands when materials are chosen for how they behave, not only how they appear.

Chapter 9

Production Failures

There is a moment in every façade project when the design finally leaves the architect's world and enters the factory floor.

- The drawings become metal sheets.
- The geometry becomes folds.
- The vision becomes a physical surface that can be bent, cut, polished, coated, and assembled.
- This is the moment where architecture and industry must speak the same language.

And it is also the moment where most façade failures are born.

A façade can be brilliantly conceptualised, flawlessly planned, and intelligently specified, and still fail if the production process does not translate the design's intentions with discipline. Factories carry their own logic, their own constraints, their own rhythms, and their own behaviours. When architects do not understand these behaviours, they unknowingly design façades that production struggles to execute with the required precision.

The mistakes that happen in production are almost invisible during early reviews.

They show themselves slowly, on-site, when the panels arrive.

- One panel looks slightly duller than the next.
- The corner of a bend does not close perfectly.
- A joint alignment breaks by just a few millimeters. A perforated pattern appears inconsistent when spread across multiple
- panels.
- A colour shift becomes apparent under natural light.
- Curves lose discipline.
- Folds lose sharpness.

Suddenly, the façade no longer looks like the renders. It looks like an approximation.

This chapter exposes the unseen reasons behind those approximations. These are the failures that take place before installation, before logistics, before site conditions, and long before the architect realises something has gone wrong. Understanding them gives

you the power to predict, question, control, and correct production before it becomes a problem.

The Failure of Inconsistent Bending

Bending is one of the most essential processes in shaping metal panels. It defines their geometry, stiffness, and overall expression. Yet bending is also one of the most delicate operations in production. A bend that is one or two degrees off can disrupt the entire alignment of a façade. A fold that is not sharp enough can destroy the intended shadow behaviour. A curve that is not uniform across a series of panels can break the continuity of a design.

Several variables affect bending consistency. The alloy, thickness, temper, die condition, machine calibration, operator experience, and even the weather inside the factory influence how metal responds to force. If these variables are not controlled with precision, each panel begins to behave slightly differently. This is how façades develop subtle undulations that appear only when multiple panels are installed together.

Bending must be treated as a controlled craft. Every angle, every fold, every curve must be tested, repeated, calibrated, and verified. When production fails to maintain consistency, the façade carries the evidence forever.

The Failure of Burrs, Sharp Edges, and Laser Marks

When panels are cut, they often develop burrs along the edges. These small, sharp protrusions may seem insignificant in the factory, but they become disastrous during coating. Left unaddressed, they also pose a safety risk during installation and later maintenance, where sharp edges can easily cause cuts to hands and fingers. Similarly, laser marks left on the surface during cutting can become permanently visible after coating if they are not cleaned properly.

The surface cleanliness determines whether the façade will look polished or careless. A façade with even a few panels showing rough edges or visible cutting marks immediately loses its premium quality. Cleaning is not an optional step in production. It is a stage where craftsmanship and discipline reveal themselves.

If the surface is not perfectly prepared, the coating will expose every flaw rather than hide it.

The Failure of Closed Corners and Improper Corner Detailing

Corners are the most expressive parts of a façade. They reveal geometry, precision, and craftsmanship. They must close elegantly, without too much gap and without too much tension. They must express the architect's intention perfectly. Yet corners are also where production struggles the most.

Improper corner forming happens when the bending logic does not match the panel's depth, thickness, or intended appearance. Closed corners require careful notch design, precise cutting, accurate bending, and press fitting. If any of these steps are rushed, the corner becomes a visible weakness. It may bulge, show a hairline gap, or fail to align with adjacent panels.

Corners demand mastery. They demand prototypes. They demand strict quality checks. When corners fail, the façade feels unfinished even if every other panel is flawless.

The Failure of Bend Relief Understanding

Every panel that includes folds or cut-outs is affected by how stress redistributes during bending. Bend relief is the mechanism that allows this stress to release in a controlled way, preventing tearing, distortion, and stress marks at fold edges.

When relief conditions are not resolved within the panel geometry, material stress concentrates at vulnerable points. Cracking or distortion may not be immediately visible during forming, but it often reveals itself later, appearing on site as subtle surface flaws that disrupt the clarity and purity of the form.

Bend relief is not an engineering detail in isolation. It is part of the material's natural response to deformation. Metal does not bend uniformly. It reallocates tension, compresses edges, and reacts to geometry in predictable ways. When this behaviour is accommodated, folds remain clean and stable. When it is not, the façade begins to express internal stress through visible imperfections.

The façade does not choose whether to reveal this stress. It simply responds to how the panel was allowed to bend.

The Failure of Notching Discipline

Notching is the process of removing small sections of metal to allow folds, intersections, and complex panel shapes. Notching must be executed with absolute precision. If it is too large, the panel loses strength. If it is too small, the panel buckles. If it is irregular, the corner transitions look sloppy. If it is rough, the coating exposes the imperfection.

Most architects never see the notching process. They only see the outcome on-site, often without knowing why a certain edge looks untidy. Notching is where the façade's eventual cleanliness and discipline are determined long before installation.

A panel that is notched with care will behave with composure. A panel that is notched carelessly will embarrass the façade.

The Failure of Surface Cleanliness Before Coating

The coating stage is one of the most misunderstood yet crucial aspects of façade production. Coating determines the façade's colour, texture, feel, and longevity. But the coating process is only as good as the surface it is applied to. If the metal surface carries dust, oil, fingerprints, micro scratches, moisture, or chemical residue, the coating will amplify these imperfections.

Many production failures occur because coatings are applied over surfaces that were not treated with the seriousness they deserve. The result is patchiness, bubbling, orange peel effect, streaking, colour variation, or early fading. Architects notice these imperfections painfully on the day the panels arrive on-site, when it is too late to intervene.

Clean metal welcomes coating. Contaminated metal destroys it. There is no shortcut.

The Failure of Colour Inconsistency Across Batches

One of the most heartbreaking production failures is colour variation. A façade designed to look seamless suddenly appears patchy when installed because the panels do not share the same colour tone. This happens for several reasons: multiple production batches, inconsistent coating thickness, variations in curing temperature, ageing of powder in storage, or differences in surface preparation.

Colour inconsistency is not a small flaw. It changes the entire identity of the façade. A building intended to look sharp and uniform suddenly appears careless. The issue becomes especially visible under sunlight, where panels reflect different shades of the same colour.

The only way to prevent this is through strict batch control, consistent coating processes, and full-scale mockups that reveal variation early. When production respects consistency, the façade feels calm and harmonious. When it does not, the façade feels agitated.

The Failure of Uneven Distribution of Coating

Even if the colour is correct, uneven application of powder or paint leads to subtle texture variations. Corners may appear slightly thicker. Flat surfaces may appear thinner. Edges may catch more powder than faces. When light hits the façade, these inconsistencies betray themselves.

Smoothness is not an aesthetic luxury. It is a sign of competence. A façade with uneven coating reveals the production team's lack of discipline instantly, no matter how beautiful the design is.

Coating must be applied like an artist applying a glaze. It must be controlled, intentional, and even. Anything less reduces the façade's refinement.

The Failure of Improper Handling

Panels are fragile before they are installed. They scratch easily. They dent easily. They bend under their own weight if lifted incorrectly. They pick up fingerprints, cloth fibers, and marks from suction cups. The site team often receives panels that were damaged not during installation, but during production and transport.

Handling discipline is not an optional part of production. It is the respect a facility shows toward the architect's design. A panel that is handled without care carries scars that no amount of installation precision can hide.

When the handling process is flawed, the panels arrive defeated.

The Failure of Weak Packing and Packaging

Packing determines how the panels survive the journey to the site. Panels that are packed without protection rub against each other, scratch during transit, or gather moisture. If panels are stacked improperly, the weight distribution causes warping.

The quality of packing determines whether the façade will look fresh or damaged before installation even begins.

A panel that arrives safely is a panel that was respected in production.

The Failure of Not Coating Both Sides When Required

In many façade systems, only the front face is coated while the back face is left untreated. This becomes a problem when the back side is visible through glass or through perforations. It also becomes a problem when the panel expands or contracts unevenly due to differing heat absorption on the two sides.

Certain façade conditions require both sides to be coated. When production fails to recognise this, the façade expresses uneven behaviour and inconsistent appearance.

> "Production is not where the façade is built. It is where the truth about your design is revealed. If production is weak, even a brilliant design looks ordinary."
>
> **- Ankur Hora, Founder of MetaMask**

Production is where architecture becomes real. And real architecture demands discipline.

KEY TAKEAWAYS FOR ARCHITECTS

- Most façade failures originate in production long before installation begins. Inconsistent bending, poor notching, weak corner detailing, and unclean surfaces all compromise the final outcome.
- Coating quality depends entirely on surface preparation, batch consistency, and careful application.
- Handling and packing are not minor steps; they determine whether the façade arrives in a condition worthy of installation.

A façade that looks refined on-site is always produced in a factory that respects precision, consistency, and discipline.

Chapter 10

Execution Failures

Execution is where architecture is tested. It is the moment when the drawings stop being promises and start becoming reality. It is the stage where the smallest oversight becomes visible, the most innocent assumption becomes expensive, and the most elegant design becomes vulnerable. Every façade stands on the shoulders of execution. If execution is weak, the façade collapses, not structurally, but visually, emotionally, and experientially.

Architects are often forced to watch their clean drawings drift into improvisation. They see joints that do not align, corners that do not close, lighting lines that look like last minute additions, and panels that carry dents or marks that were never meant to exist.

They see decisions being made on-site that were never part of the design intent. They see the façade become a negotiation between time, skill, and convenience rather than a reflection of their vision.

This chapter explains why this happens. Not in the vague, philosophical sense. But in the exact, practical, technical sense. You will understand the realities of site work that no one explains to architects, even though these realities determine the fate of almost every façade.

Where Execution Begins to Slip

Execution rarely unravels because of a single dramatic failure. It slows, stretches, and fragments over time. In many façade projects, the earliest signs of slippage appear not on site, but upstream, within fabrication and coordination timelines.

Metal façade manufacturing is a capacity-intensive process. Many manufacturers operate with multiple overlapping projects, shared production lines, and stretched installation teams. When workload exceeds manageable limits, priorities shift. Fabrication schedules slide. Coordination weakens. Decisions are deferred. Timelines begin to compress downstream.

Delays at the manufacturing or project management level ripple forward. Installation windows shrink. Site sequencing becomes reactive. Panels arrive late or out of order. Site teams are forced to work around incomplete deliveries, accelerating some tasks while postponing others. Precision work begins to absorb time pressure it was never designed to handle.

This environment creates friction, not because intent is unclear, but because execution is asked to move faster than systems allow. Alignment checks are rushed. Handling discipline weakens. Interfaces are resolved on the fly. Small compromises accumulate quietly.

Most façade delays trace back to capacity and coordination gaps rather than design complexity. When fabrication planning, project management, and site integration are stretched thin, even well-designed façades struggle to maintain rhythm. Execution does not collapse. It drifts.

The Absence of Panel Sequencing

Panel sequencing is one of the most critical disciplines in façade execution. Panels are not meant to be installed randomly. Their order is defined by joint logic, alignment rhythm, structural anchoring, and visual continuity. When sequencing is unclear or inconsistently followed, the façade begins to behave like an unsolved puzzle. Panels drift out of alignment. Joints lose rhythm. Corners feel unresolved. Shadows fall unpredictably.

Clear sequencing allows the façade to grow in a controlled direction. It ensures that visual lines remain continuous, that joints behave consistently, and that the substructure supports each panel under the correct conditions. Sequencing is not just about order. It is about preserving intent as the façade takes physical form.

Breakdowns typically occur when sequencing intent is not communicated clearly to the fabrication and installation teams at site, or when that sequence is not enforced consistently during execution. In such situations, installation often begins based on convenience rather than logic. Panels may start getting installed from multiple directions at once, creating alignment conflicts that cannot be corrected later.

Metal façades, in particular, demand disciplined sequencing. Most systems are designed to be installed progressively from one direction to another. When this logic is disrupted, the façade loses the rhythm it was designed to carry, even if every individual panel is fabricated correctly.

Sequence is the choreography of execution. When it is clearly defined, communicated, and followed, the façade moves as one continuous composition. Without it, even a well-designed system struggles to hold together.

The Bad Habit of Improvised Joinery

Joinery details are the personality of a façade. They define its character in sunlight. They determine how clean the façade looks from near and far. Yet joinery is often improvised on-site because the installers run into conditions they did not anticipate. A bracket is slightly out of place. A substructure is a few millimeters off. A beam edge is not finished straight. A lighting cable blocks a flush fit. When this happens, installers adjust the joinery quietly. They create micro-gaps that were never meant to exist.

Most architects never learn about these adjustments until the façade is complete. And by then, the rhythm of the joints is already broken.

When joinery is improvised, the façade carries a visual tension that never goes away. It loses sharpness. It loses discipline. It loses its architectural confidence.

The Universal Problem of Exposed Joinery

Exposed fasteners are one of the clearest signs that execution discipline was abandoned. A façade designed to appear seamless suddenly displays screws or rivets that should have been concealed. This usually happens when the substructure was not aligned properly during bracket installation. Installers, in a hurry to complete the area, choose visible fixing methods rather than reworking the substructure.

Exposed joinery tells the truth about the site. It reveals where the contractor chose convenience over craftsmanship. It reveals where the supervision was weak. It reveals where the design intent was not protected.

A façade should express its beauty quietly. Visible screws make it speak too loudly, and for the wrong reasons.

The Failure of Site Measurement Discipline

Execution depends on measurement accuracy. Even small deviations compound rapidly across a façade. At the site level, measurement responsibility is often delegated to execution or measurement teams who may not be fully aware of how critical even a 5 mm deviation can be to alignment, joint continuity, and overall façade rhythm.

Under schedule pressure, such deviations are sometimes treated as acceptable tolerances. In reality, a few millimetres at one point can translate into visible misalignment across multiple panels, causing joints to drift, corners to misread, and visual lines to break.

Façade systems respond precisely to measurement accuracy. When deviations are understood and controlled, the elevation remains composed. When their impact is underestimated, the façade begins to express inconsistency that cannot be corrected later. They assume the next panel will hide the previous flaw.

These assumptions add up. They accumulate into a façade where the eye senses inconsistency even when exact measurements do not reveal it. Architecture is visual

mathematics. It does not forgive even the smallest deviation when repeated across dozens of panels.

Measurement discipline is the backbone of execution. Without it, the façade loses its order.

The Painful Problem of Missing Fillers

Fillers are the unsung heroes of façade execution. They hide internal gaps, support edges, block light leaks, and protect the façade from dust and insects. When fillers are missing, loosely installed, or misaligned, the façade develops visible inconsistencies. Light leaks appear around joints. Dust accumulates behind panels. Edges feel hollow. Corners become weak.

When applied correctly, fillers also play a critical role in controlling water ingress. By sealing gaps, joints, and micro-cracks along panel edges and interfaces, they help prevent moisture from penetrating the building envelope. This sealing action significantly reduces the risk of seepage, dampness, and long-term water damage. In this sense, fillers are not cosmetic accessories but an essential part of the façade's waterproofing strategy, protecting both performance and durability.

Fillers may seem like minor details, but they define the façade's emotional experience. A façade without proper fillers feels unfinished no matter how well the panels are aligned.

Architects often blame themselves or the material when they see these issues on-site. In reality, these issues originate from poor execution discipline.

The Failure of Slope Logic Leading to Water Ingress

Water is merciless. It finds every weakness. Even the smallest reverse slope becomes an entry point. When panels are installed without respecting slope logic, water enters behind the façade. It dampens the wall. It travels through gaps. It causes stains. It affects insulation. And eventually, it expresses itself on the exterior.

Slope is not a civil detail. Slope belongs to the façade. It determines whether water flows away from the building or into it.

Reverse slopes are among the costliest execution errors. They are not visible in renders or drawings. They appear only on-site when a small alignment mistake changes the angle of a panel or flashing.

A façade can survive almost any challenge except water entering behind it. Water never forgives poor execution.

The Failure to Provide Cleaning and Maintenance Access

Every façade must be maintainable. But when the façade has deep recesses, overhangs, horizontal surfaces, or perforated elements, cleaning becomes difficult. Dust accumulates. Stains form. Surfaces weather unevenly. A façade that cannot be cleaned gracefully becomes a façade that ages poorly.

During execution, if access points, hooks, maintenance openings, or safe cleaning paths are not created, the building carries a long-term flaw that can never be corrected.

Maintenance is not an afterthought. It must be part of the execution sequence.

The Constant Threat of Scratches and Handling Damage

Most façade panels that arrive scratched were not damaged in the factory. They were damaged on-site. Workers move the scaffolding. Welders work nearby. Tools fall. Cables swing. Dust embeds itself into soft coatings. Suction cups leave marks. Panels brush against rebar bundles or concrete edges.

Handling damage is often dismissed as inevitable. It is not. It is the result of poor supervision, lack of awareness, and weak respect for the façade.

A single scratch can change the perception of an entire elevation. That is how sensitive façades are to execution quality.

The Problem of Missing Panels, Delayed Panels, and Wrong Panels

Every site faces delays. But many delays are caused not by production or logistics but by execution mismanagement. Panels get misplaced. Wrong panels get installed.

Missing panels halt the sequence. The work slows down not because the façade is complex, but because the site is disorganised.

This creates a chain reaction. Installers skip areas. Sequencing breaks. Joints misalign. Stress builds. Corners start losing refinement. The façade loses its flow.

Execution success often depends on something as simple as site discipline.

The Failure of Edge Treatment After Cutting

Whenever panels are cut on-site, their raw edges must be treated. Raw edges expose the metal to the environment. They create points where moisture enters, corrosion begins, and finishes degrade. They also reveal unfinished metal that contrasts sharply with the façade's coated surfaces.

When installers skip edge treatment because of time pressure, the façade loses its longevity and its visual coherence. The edge becomes a weak point that grows more visible over time.

"Execution is not construction. Execution is the art of protecting the architect's intent from the chaos of the site."

- Ankur Hora, Founder of MetaMask

A façade succeeds when execution respects intention. Without that respect, no material, no system, and no design can hold alignment.

KEY TAKEAWAYS

- Execution is where the façade either becomes architecture or collapses into improvisation.
- Sequencing, joinery discipline, measurement consistency, and slope logic determine success.
- Scratches, dents, poor handling, missing fillers, and exposed fixings ruin façade purity. Lighting and maintenance access must be executed with the same seriousness as panel installation.

A well-executed façade is the result of supervision, discipline, and protection of the design intent at every step.

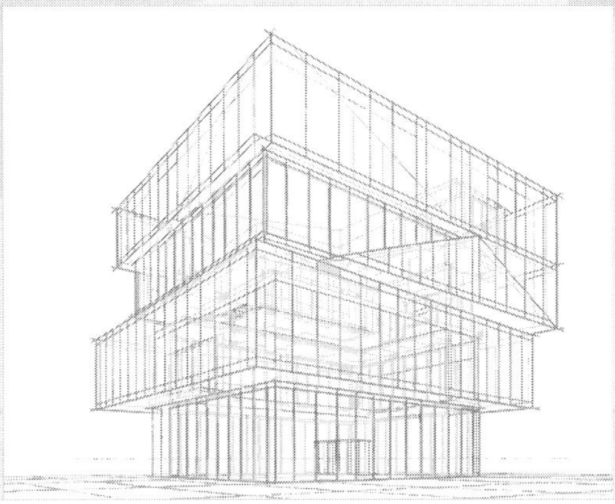

PART IV
The MetaMask Story

Chapter 11

Why MetaMask Exists

Façade outcomes rarely fail because of design intent.

They drift because intent passes through too many hands, timelines, and interpretations before it becomes built reality.

Between the architect's drawing and the finished façade lies a long and fragile journey. This journey moves through planning coordination, material selection, detailing, fabrication, logistics, site sequencing, and installation under real conditions. Each stage introduces variables. Each variable carries the potential to quietly distort what was originally imagined.

The façade does not collapse at one point.

It erodes gradually.

MetaMask exists in this gap.

Not as a replacement for architects.

Not as a challenger to design authorship.

But as a system created to protect façade intent as it moves from concept to construction.

The Gap No One Owned

Traditionally, façade responsibility has been fragmented.

Design intent is established in the studio.

Engineering logic is developed in parallel.

Fabrication decisions are made under production pressures.

Installation unfolds under site constraints and shifting timelines.

Each participant performs their role competently.

Yet no single entity is responsible for **continuity** across the entire façade lifecycle.

What often goes missing is not expertise, but ownership of the transitions between stages.

MetaMask was formed to address exactly this absence.

A System, Not a Vendor

MetaMask does not operate as a product supplier or a fabrication house in isolation. It operates as a façade systems partner.

The focus is not on selling materials.

The focus is on understanding how design intent behaves when it encounters material behaviour, manufacturing realities, sequencing logic, and site execution.

Every façade challenge MetaMask addresses is approached through three lenses:

- Behaviour at scale
- Continuity across stages
- Risk visibility before execution

This approach allows potential issues to be identified when they are still design decisions, not site crises.

Where MetaMask Adds Value

MetaMask engages at points where façade projects typically lose clarity:

- Translating architectural intent into fabrication-ready logic without diluting expression

- Aligning material behaviour with form, geometry, and detailing
- Coordinating façade systems with structure, MEP, waterproofing, and lighting early
- Bringing sequencing, tolerances, and execution realities into planning conversations
- Ensuring that what is fabricated can actually be installed as intended

The role is not to redesign.

The role is to **preserve**.

Protecting Intent Through Execution

Execution pressure is unavoidable.

Timelines compress.

Site conditions evolve.

Multiple teams overlap.

In this environment, façades need systems that can absorb complexity without losing coherence.

MetaMask's involvement focuses on:

- Clarity of detailing
- Discipline of sequencing
- Realism of tolerances
- Alignment of responsibilities

This reduces improvisation on site and allows installation teams to work with intent rather than correction.

Why This Matters

Architectural façades today are expected to do more than enclose buildings. They carry identity.

They manage the environment.

They communicate intent at an urban scale.

As façades become more expressive and technically demanding, the margin for error narrows.

MetaMask exists because modern façades require deeper coordination, earlier visibility of risk, continuity across disciplines, and stewardship beyond drawings

A Quiet Role by Design

MetaMask does not seek visibility over authorship.

The façade should always read as the architect's work.

When a façade performs well, it should feel effortless.

When it ages gracefully, it should feel inevitable.

When it holds together under real conditions, it should feel intentional. MetaMask's role is successful when it is invisible.

CLOSING PERSPECTIVE

Façade excellence is rarely about bold gestures alone.

It is about discipline, alignment, and foresight carried consistently across the project lifecycle.

MetaMask exists to provide that continuity.

Not to control design.

But to ensure that design survives the journey.

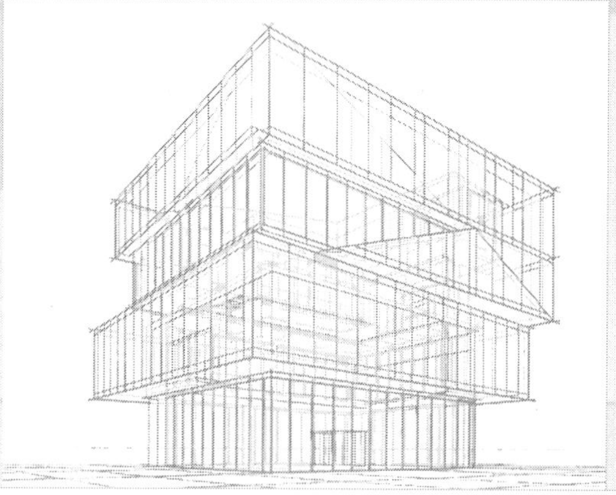

PART V
Real Projects, Real Lessons

Chapter 12

Case Studies: When Design Was Saved And When It Wasn't

Architecture does not fail because of lack of ideas.

It fails when intent is not protected once drawings meet reality.

The earlier parts of this book explored how design weakens, how form drifts, how material behaves, and how execution leaves permanent evidence. Part V brings those ideas into the real world through projects executed by the Meta Mask team under Ankur Hora's leadership.

These are not conceptual studies. They are not theoretical examples. They are not ideal conditions.

They are commercial projects with active services, tight timelines, coordination pressure, budget constraints, and site realities.

What makes them relevant is not scale or spectacle. It is control.

Why These Projects Matter

Each project in this part demonstrates a simple truth. Façade quality is decided early, defended deliberately, and executed with method.

These projects show how architectural intent can survive:

✓ heavy services behind the façade

✓ highly visible urban locations

✓ façades experienced in motion

✓ tight execution timelines

They are included to show how principles become practice.

Case Study 1

Service-Heavy Buildings Without Visual Compromise

DLF Downtown Commercial Project near Cyber Hub, Delhi–Jaipur Highway

This project involved a commercial building with three active hot kitchens located directly behind the façade. Exhaust systems, ducts, and mechanical services needed to function fully while remaining visually concealed.

The architectural challenge was not simply hiding services.

It was doing so without flattening the elevation, breaking proportions, or introducing patchwork solutions that diluted the design.

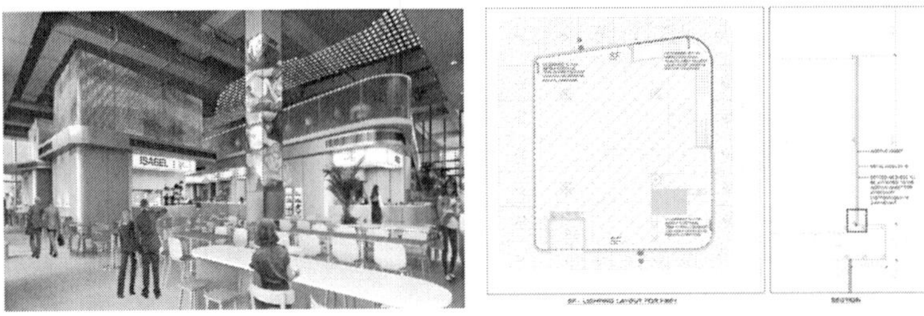

Data received from the clint

The architect also required a façade surface that could express two tones on a single plane, without artificial colour breaks or layered panels.

Meta Mask proposed a patterned aluminium façade system where tonal variation emerged from geometry and light interaction rather than applied colour. The façade treated colour as a result of form, not paint.

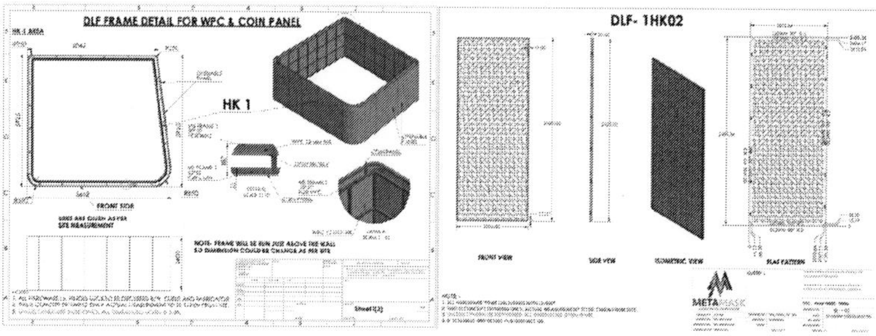

Technical Details by metamask

Once the pattern and colour palette were approved, execution followed the approved design without deviation. The façade covered approximately 1800 square feet using 2 mm aluminium panels, balancing precision with durability.

The final outcome

Concealed services cleanly, preserved ventilation performance, and delivered a composed façade that remained faithful to the architect's original intent.

What This Project Demonstrates

When façade logic and services are resolved together at the design stage, execution does not need to compensate later.

> **"When the façade is planned as a system, even complex services stop being a visual problem."**

Case Study 2

Designing for Movement, Not Just Appearance

Aditya developers Metro-Facing Commercial Complex, Sector 501, Noida

This project faced a metro corridor and a primary road, meaning the façade was experienced largely in motion. The brief was clear. The elevation needed to feel dynamic, not static.

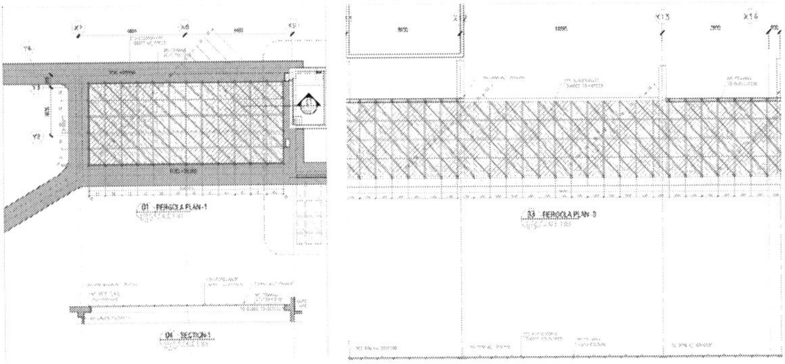

Data received from the client

The requirement was not visual noise.

It was controlled variation.

Meta Mask proposed a parametric aluminium façade

system composed of angled metal flaps arranged in a deliberate sequence. The geometry was designed to change perception based on viewing angle and light conditions.

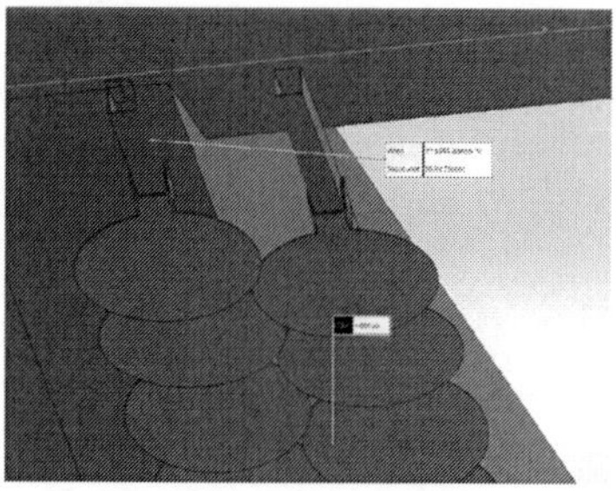

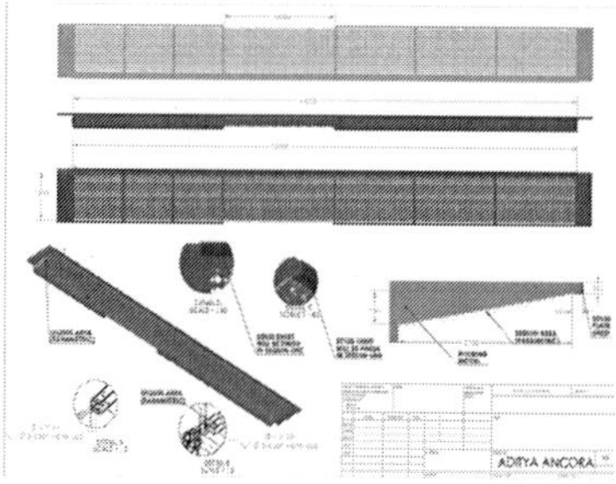

Technical Details by metamask

The system used 2 mm aluminium elements mounted on a tubular framework. A gold-toned powder-coated finish was selected to enhance reflection without visual harshness.

The façade covered approximately 5,000 square feet and was completed within two months. Following completion, the client extended the scope, applying the same system to additional areas.

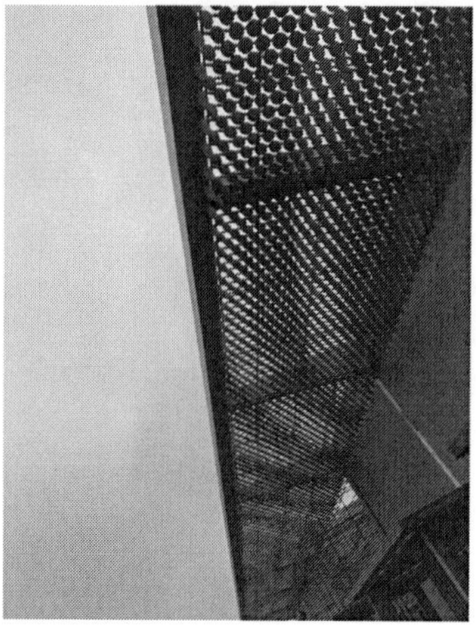

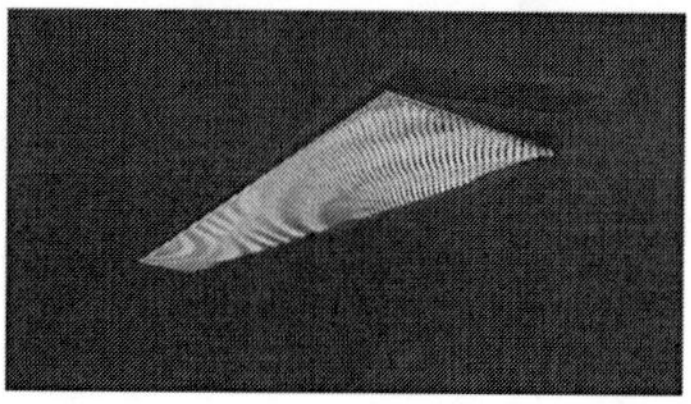

The final outcome

The façade performs strongest when viewed in motion, exactly as intended.

What This Project Demonstrates

When context defines how a building is seen, the façade must respond to movement, not just appearance.

What These Projects Prove

These projects are not presented as achievements. They are presented as evidence.

They show what happens when:

→ intent is resolved early

→ geometry is protected

→ material behaviour is understood

→ execution is controlled

Architecture survives when it is defended with method, not assumptions.

Key Takeaways

Complex façades fail when method is weak but succeed when process is disciplined.

The world's most iconic metal façades were built not through artistic freedom but through engineering clarity.

Real failures in high-rise buildings show that fixings, joints, and maintenance are not optional tasks but safety obligations.

Mockups change decisions. They save the façade before the façade exists.

Architecture survives when the architect protects intention with evidence, not assumptions.

Now You Have Two Choices...

You can move forward with whoever sold you the last façade.

Rely on familiar products. Familiar processes. Familiar outcomes.

Or you can place a system on your side.

One that protects design intent before timelines tighten, coordination fragments, and execution pressure sets in.

The difference is not in how the façade looks on paper.

It is in how faithfully it gets built.

If the next façade is expected to stand out, perform, and endure, the choice must be made early.

Have the right system on your side before execution begins.

A project discovery conversation can be initiated via the QR code below.

A New Way to Build
Architecture That Survives Execution

Every architect begins with intention. A line on paper. A surface imagined. A form waiting to become real. But intention alone cannot survive the journey from drawing to building. It needs structure. It needs discipline. It needs partners who understand that a façade is not decoration. It is the identity of a building. It is the part of the architecture that meets the world first and stays with the world the longest.

Metal façades offer possibilities no other material can. They fold, bend, curve, perforate, glow, and express identity with precision. But they also demand respect. They demand clarity in planning, accuracy in production, and discipline in execution. When these three stages align, the façade becomes a truthful extension of the architect's mind. When they fail, the façade becomes a reminder of compromises that should never have been accepted.

This book is not about metal alone.

- It is about the mindset required to turn architecture into reality.
- It is about protecting design from erosion. It is about giving architects the tools to insist on what their drawings truly mean.
- It is about proving that when a method supports imagination, even the most ambitious façade can be delivered exactly as intended.

The future belongs to buildings that are honest in daylight and unforgettable at night.

- Buildings that use geometry and light to speak.
- Buildings that respect material behaviour.
- Buildings that express identity with confidence.
- Buildings where architecture and execution are not two different conversations.

May this book remind every architect that their design deserves a team that protects it. A façade deserves clarity. A building deserves discipline. And the city deserves architecture that stands with integrity.

The journey from concept to completion will never be simple. But it can be precise. It can be intelligent. And it can be worthy of the idea that started it.

Now You Have Two Choices...

You can move forward with whoever sold you the last façade.

Rely on familiar products. Familiar processes. Familiar outcomes.

Or you can place a system on your side.

One that protects design intent before timelines tighten, coordination fragments, and execution pressure sets in.

The difference is not in how the façade looks on paper.

It is in how faithfully it gets built.

If the next façade is expected to stand out, perform, and endure, the choice must be made early.

Have the right system on your side before execution begins.

A project discovery conversation can be initiated via the QR code below.

ACKNOWLEDGMENTS

This book is the result of countless conversations with architects, fabricators, site engineers, and project leaders who have lived the realities described in these pages.

Their honesty, experience, and willingness to share their successes and failures shaped the insights you now hold.

A special note of gratitude to the MetaMask fabrication and engineering teams. Their commitment to technical clarity, process discipline, and material excellence has created the foundation for every principle discussed in this book.

To the architects who push the boundaries of what metal can express. Thank you for trusting materials to carry your ideas. Your ambition is the reason façades continue to evolve.

To the project managers and site teams who bring these ideas to life with patience and precision. Your work is the final translation of design into reality.

And to the readers, especially young architects and designers. May this book help you protect your vision and demand the quality your work deserves.

Thank you for believing in a future where façades are not afterthoughts but expressions of intention.

A CLOSING NOTE FROM METAMASK

At MetaMask, we believe metal is more than a material. It is a language.

When understood correctly, it can express identity, depth, light, geometry, and intent with unmatched clarity. But metal does not tolerate guesswork. It rewards accuracy. It respects discipline. And it reveals the truth of every decision made during planning, production, and execution.

Our mission has always been simple.

- To support architects in building façades that survive the journey from idea to actuality. To engineer panels that behave predictably.
- To bring a level of method and precision that protects the design.
- To ensure the façade that stands on-site feels exactly like the one imagined in the studio.

This book is an extension of that mission. It is a commitment to transparency, education, and excellence.

Whether your project demands complex geometry, subtle expression, or seamless material fusion, we stand ready to support your intention with the technical depth it deserves.

Thank you for letting MetaMask be a part of your architecture.

We look forward to building the future with you.

linkedin

Instagram

Youtube

Facebook

website